# A CUDDLE of CATS

## Rhymes and Recollections

Heather Cook
Photographs by Roger Cook

Matador
9 Priory Business Park,
Wistow Road, Kibworth Beauchamp,
Leicestershire. LE8 0RX
Tel: 0116 279 2299
Email: books@troubador.co.uk
Web: www.troubador.co.uk/matador
Twitter: @matadorbooks

ISBN 978 1785893 889

British Library Cataloguing in Publication Data.
A catalogue record for this book is available from the British Library.

Printed and bound in the UK by TJ International, Padstow, Cornwall
Typeset in 11pt Aldine401 BT by Troubador Publishing Ltd, Leicester, UK

Matador is an imprint of Troubador Publishing Ltd

*This book is dedicated to all the unsung heroes who care about animals; not just the people who work for established charities with like-minded folk around them to support them when things get tough, but the thousands of kind souls who do their best to help a needy animal in all sorts of difficult and often dangerous circumstances. These people often have no recognition or thanks from their fellow humans. Indeed, they often encounter verbal abuse and physical threats, but the difference they make to the animals they help is immeasurable.*

## ALSO BY HEATHER COOK

*Evie's Diary*
*Paws for Thought*
*From Sidcup with Purrs*
*The Old, the Mad and the Wobbly*

# INTRODUCTION

I know it's a silly title! The correct name for a gathering of cats is, of course, a 'clowder', but I think a 'cuddle' is so much more appropriate and so will you if like me you are reduced to an emotional jelly by the sight of two cats snoozing away the hours, limbs and tails entwined, chirruping with sleepy surprise when a paw inadvertently digs into a softer part of their anatomy.

Other names could also be quite fitting, including a 'cacophony' of cats, or even a 'quirkiness', but 'cuddle' wins the day for me.

That said, some of the poems in this collection feature cats who keep their cuddliness well hidden, such as Spitfire, the ancient feral, who has treasured her wildness for 15 years, remaining as ungrateful and proud as the day she arrived. Or the demon kitten, who delights in making dogs' lives a misery and gets away with it, or Tiny Trixie-Tribble, the heat-seeking missile.

But even these characters have their cuddly moments, even if it's not with us. Spitfire loved her old friend Delilah, a long-haired dolly-bird of a cat with no detectable brain, and mourned her passing; demon kittens have a habit of collapsing in a heap anywhere, anytime, adopting any number of winsome poses and Tiny has times when she just must have a cuddle – usually at the most inconvenient times, but that's cats for you.

There are some serious poems here because life does inevitably have a serious side, but I hope you'll find plenty to smile about. Above all, I hope that you will feel that the contents of this book reflect in some small way the amazing beauty and fascination of this wonderful animal.

*Heather Cook*

# Why?

*Does it really matter?*
*Why do we need to care?*
*When the world is full of worry,*
*Disappointment and despair?*
*What about the children*
*Deprived of food and health?*
*Surely we should care for them*
*With any surplus wealth?*
*And anyway, the problem's huge;*
*What difference can we make?*
*This is a cold old world, my friend,*
*With much less give than take.*
*So what is one more hungry stray,*
*Unwanted, sad and thin?*
*How can it really matter?*
*Perhaps it does – to him.*

# Cathedral Cats

We visited Salisbury Cathedral one afternoon in late October on a wonderfully still day when the leaves were shining like russet jewels against a Wedgewood sky. We were blinking as we emerged from the splendour and gloom of the Cathedral into that glorious autumn sunlight.

As I was gazing at the peaceful scene, my husband touched my arm and pointed across the lush grass. At first I couldn't see what had caught his attention, but soon I realised as a portly black cat strolled into view, a mouse clamped in its jaws. As it approached, it dropped the mouse – which rapidly pulled itself together and scampered off into the bushes – and flicked its tail into a vertical plume by way of a greeting. How I envy cats their ability to cut through all the embarrassment of not being able to remember names, or what indisposition somebody was suffering from when paths last crossed by the simple expedient of sticking their tails in the air.

Our new friend wove around our legs politely, but not ingratiatingly, and I reflected how appropriate cats are to the environs of a Cathedral. Their gracefulness and air of quiet containment equip them so appropriately for the job. Cats can always manage to look as if they are thinking deep thoughts even though they are probably only reflecting on the inadequacy of the last meal, or considering whether they should stay out late to worry their owners, who appear to have become rather complacent of late.

The time he spent with us was judged to perfection. Any longer would have meant we had to rush for the train; a shorter conversation could have seemed unduly brusque.

The thought of spaniels and terriers, charging round the place, snatching up hymn books and ramming them into visitors' legs would really be too much to bear in such a considered environment. Dogs are so much better suited to romping on beaches and digging holes on golf courses.

*In a cathedral? A dog? I think not.*
*Huffing and puffing – it would be quite odd*
*To have something so very common and rude*
*Piddling and barging about in the pews;*
*Picking up hymn books and wolfing down trash –*
*Dogs are predictable, smelly and brash.*
*But cats in cathedrals – that sounds much better*
*Than slobbering spaniels and spirited setters.*
*Cats lurk in bookshops or in the refectory,*
*Snoozing on garments stored in the vestry.*
*Cats move in a world of silkiest whispers,*
*Leaving the dogs to fetch God his slippers.*

# The New Cat Door

It has always amused me to see how cats can over-react so ridiculously to things that any reasonable creature would take in its stride. Moving a chair or table a matter of inches can produce outrage, while the replacement of an ancient cat flap is enough to make a cat think about leaving home – if only it could bring itself to use the new cat door, of course.

Thinking our cats would be thrilled to have a new, see-through cat flap in place of the ancient rubber affair, we were a bit miffed to encounter panicky stares followed by a point blank refusal to use the wretched thing.

The article I had read said that cats like to see if there is anything lurking outside before they venture out, which sounded sensible, but the author of this valuable advice had failed to take account of Sooty's nose, which assumed trunk-like proportions when viewed through the flap.

## Paw Note

At considerable expense a few years ago, I had a cat flap put into a double glazed unit at the rear of the property so that our intrepid felines could venture into the back garden without the inconvenience of having to walk all the way round from the front exit.

Almost immediately, we adopted a succession of disabled and elderly cats, who we decided should not be allowed out without supervision, so both cat flaps are now securely boarded up, their only function now being to allow a bracing draught to whip playfully round our legs on winter nights.

## The New Cat Door – Fluffy Speaks Out

*I used to have an old cat door –*
*The flap was scratched and black,*
*But then they fixed a see-through one*
*That smacked me on the back.*
*One day, about to hurtle through*
*At twice the speed of lightning,*
*I caught a glimpse of Sooty's nose,*
*Magnified and frightening.*
*When his nose grew quite so large*
*I'm not entirely sure,*
*But it returned to normal size*
*When they removed that door.*

## Miss Tiny Trixie-Tribble

It's strange how some of the best things in life come about, not as a result of astute planning or hard work, but by simply being in the right place at the right time and seizing the moment.

This was certainly how our amazing little cat, Tiny Trixie-Tribble, came into our lives. She has written a book, From Sidcup with Purrs, which tells her story, so suffice it to say that she was a stray who came to live with us after spending three years in a veterinary surgery in Sidcup.

Tiny is brimming over with fun and playfulness. She definitely doesn't think of herself as a cat and really can't be bothered with the other felines in the family. She is a Pets as Therapy cat and loves visiting the residents in various homes for the elderly, sitting on laps and enjoying all the fuss. Although she is a lively little girl, Tiny seems to understand how frail the residents are and it certainly does my old heart good to see the joy she brings to people who have in many cases had to part with a much-loved pet when their own health meant they could no longer maintain their independence.

Tiny also enjoys accompanying me to schools and Brownie groups when I give talks on cat care, but I am only too well aware of the dangers of working with children and animals! It's very hard to keep on track when a mischievous tabby cat has sent a pile of leaflets flying across the room, or has decided that she simply must run up and down the keyboard of the piano in the corner that I was hoping she wouldn't notice.

She has been particularly useful in helping nervous children who are unused to pets to gain in confidence. Most will forget their fears as Tiny leaps after her laser light toy and jumps after the dancing fishing rod toy.

Thank you, Tiny, for coming into our lives and into the lives of so many other people – young and old.

*I'm small and striped like a humbug*
*And I swoop about like a bat;*
*I'm clever and very quick-witted*
*Running rings round the average cat.*

*I was born with a bit of brain damage*
*And my head has a slight starboard tilt;*
*I'm deaf and I'm vague about dirt trays,*
*But that's just the way that I'm built.*

*They call me a heat-seeking missile,*
*But I'm just a sweet, playful cat;*
*I bowl all the other cats over*
*And they won't forgive me for that.*

*My favourite toy is a goldfish*
*That hangs from a long springy rod.*
*It's now not looking so golden –*
*With chips it would pass off as cod.*

# A Gremlin In The Kremlin

It has always seemed very sad to me that any creature – human or animal – should have no history; I can well understand the anxiety of many adopted children to find out more about their birth parents.

More frivolously, we have always tended to invent 'histories' for the numerous cats we have adopted over the years, including Sammy the stationery clerk, who retired early when computers were introduced, and Miss Poppet, who was quite clearly a typing pool supervisor in a rather moth-eaten fur coat.

A very sad-looking Persian, who had been kept in one room for eight years by her previous weird owner, didn't even have a name when she arrived, so we called her 'Bella'. For some reason, we decided that she had been a spy in St Petersburg and she became known as St Petersburg Cloud Princess. We used to talk to her about her past adventures and she would regard us trustingly with her huge round eyes, not having a clue what we were rambling on about, but enjoying the attention nonetheless.

*The old Cold War was raging*
*In a spiteful, icy way*
*And spies were two a penny –*
*Or a rouble, I should say.*
*One special double agent,*
*Loved, admired and feared*
*Was a glamorous female Persian*
*With a fetching, wispy beard.*
*She was known as Kremlin Gremlin,*
*With eyes that could destroy;*
*She was absolutely deadly,*
*But looked just like a toy.*
*She could decode a message*
*In the time it took to blink*
*While dancing like a Cossack*
*On Kruschev's skating rink.*
*There were a lot of spies of course,*
*Like those moody British Blues,*
*Who were Russian when they fancied,*
*Wearing boots instead of shoes.*
*Gremlin hid dark secrets*
*In her long and lustrous fur*
*And if somebody challenged her*
*She'd rub her ears and purr.*
*One day she received an offer*
*Of very many dollars*
*From a handsome young American*
*Who promised diamond collars.*
*Kremlin Gremlin thought a bit,*
*Then rushed to catch the plane;*
*You may not be surprised to hear*
*She's now called White House Jane.*

# BENJY'S LAMENT

Our wonderful brain-damaged ginger boy, Benjamin Wobble, has two great interests in life. One is food and the other is bonking anything that will keep still for long enough. As Benjamin doesn't move very quickly, this generally means that a particularly fluffy bed comes in for more than its fair share of punishment. Every now and then, Bonky Bed looks very much the worse for wear and has to take a turn in the washing machine, emerging fragrant and fluffy after several cycles. The first time this happened, I proudly reintroduced Benjy to the love of his life to be met with his best 'Disgusted of Tunbridge Wells' expression. It took several days for Benjy to forgive me and for harmonious relations between Benjy and Bonky to be restored.

The only way I can stop Benjy eating everybody else's food is by putting some dishes out of his reach. This always makes me feel spiteful, but being overweight and wobbly isn't a good combination. As for his feline chums being able to snaffle anything from his own plate, Benjy scuppers any plans they might have by the simple expedient of flinging himself across the food. He obviously considers that congealing gravy on one's tum is just a small price to pay – and could come in handy as a snack later.

I didn't think I'd better write a poem about bonking, so food it is!

*I'm meant to be a squashy cat –*
*Plump and wobbly – almost fat.*
*I never was a skinny rake*
*Or a whippy racing snake.*
*My humans put me on a diet*
*And when I said that they should try it,*
*They dished me up some awful food*
*As punishment for being rude.*
*I phoned a charity for assistance,*
*Then at their concerned insistence,*
*Phoned Her Majesty for help.*
*She couldn't hear above the yelp*
*Of corgis scrapping over bones*
*Under and around her throne,*
*But thank heavens, in the end*
*She promised me that she would send*
*Some tasty morsels from the Palace*
*To provide much-needed ballast.*
*The royal parcel when it came*
*Contained some venison and game*
*Which stopped the rumbling in my tum*
*But gave me quite a windy bum.*

# WHEN THE MARTIANS LANDED

Most of the cat lovers I know – and I include myself – are fully aware of their own peculiarities, which is just as well because others waste no time in telling us how bonkers they think we are.

Sometimes though, when I catch myself being particularly daft about cats, I do make an effort to see things from a 'normal' person's point of view – or a Martian's! I also like to think how they could also become besotted with these furry creatures – a phenomenon I frequently encountered when involved in finding new homes for unwanted cats and kittens.

Couples would often come to look at cats and at that stage it would often be the woman who was the more enthusiastic of the two. The male partner would stand back, smiling indulgently, while he distanced himself from the enterprise with remarks like, 'Of course, I don't dislike cats, but it's my wife/girlfriend who really wants it.'

I would nod understandingly, secure in the knowledge that within a few days of her arrival, Fluffy would have the great lump completely under her paw. He would be telling everyone how exceptionally clever Fluffy was, as well as incredibly beautiful. His work colleagues would be glazing over as yet more photographs of Fluffy were paraded before them, while they were regaled with tales of Fluffy's latest achievements. Patting a ping-pong ball? Imagine that!

*One day the Martians landed*
*And were fair amazed*
*To see the way that humans*
*Were everywhere enslaved.*
*They worked like beavers all the time*
*And didn't have much fun*
*While all those furry things called cats*
*Slept soundly in the sun.*
*A Martian child was first to stroke*
*A spidery, fuzzy kitten*
*And soon his Martian mum and dad*
*Were absolutely smitten.*
*The humans whined and wailed, of course,*
*About their pets' disloyalty;*
*Cats don't say sorry or explain,*
*As is the way with royalty.*
*So soon old Fluffy and her mates*
*Had legged it through their flaps*
*To rub round metal ankles*
*And snooze on scaly laps.*

# PORTIA

Animals have keen survival instincts and even in domestic pets it's easy to see the ones who have reached an advanced level.

When I was finding homes for cats and kittens and had pens in my back garden, I would try to identify the one that a potential owner might be interested in adopting before the person arrived, but time and time again I would be gloriously wrong. Often, the person themselves would think they wanted a long-haired ginger kitten, but would be unaccountably smitten by a short-haired black cat of uncertain age. Sometimes they would insist they only wanted one cat, but would fall hook, line and sinker for a pair of cats that simply could not be separated. And thank goodness they did!

Some of the animals that came into our care had been through the mill. This was particularly true in my experience with kittens, who were frequently the offspring of sad, undernourished mothers and were, therefore, skinny little creatures who had fought off any number of ghastly bacterial and parasitic invasions. These babies were battle-hardened and once they began to feel better, a vulnerable human being didn't stand a chance.

There were many cats and kittens like Portia, who may have had their paws in the dirt tray, but their eyes were firmly fixed on the stars above.

*Everything she does is prettily done.*
*Even her dirt tray business is completed*
*Expeditiously and without vulgar straining.*
*She keeps her white coat in good order*
*With delicate licks of her strawberry tongue*
*And sharpens her claws with deft flexes*
*On treasured and expensive rugs.*
*Portia has not always been so pretty*
*And she has not always been Portia.*
*She was a ragged kitten, wearing noxious smells,*
*Given sanctuary by those who called her 'Snowy',*
*But the name was the least of her worries.*
*When Snowy saw her chance, she seized it*
*With four small paws and one desperate cry.*
*The woman had liked the pedigree kitten,*
*Playing so prettily in the cage next door.*
*She had cupped her hands around its tiny body*
*And spoken to it in kitten language.*
*Snowy knew that she would like to go home*
*With this soft-voiced lady and be loved.*
*She raised a fragile paw, looked into the woman's face,*
*Mewed a croaky mew and purred a rasping purr.*
*The woman put the other kitten back,*
*Knowing that someone else would love her,*
*And picked up the ragged, smelly little waif.*
*At that moment, Snowy became Portia,*
*To be loved beyond reason for the rest of her life.*

# JUST A CAT

There can't be many cat lovers who haven't encountered the stunned reactions of non-cat lovers to their devastation at the loss of their dearest furry friend. Quite why people imagine that putting their own evaluation on the appropriateness and worthiness of another person's grief is at all helpful, I really have no idea. It seems to me that if somebody were mourning the loss of a snail the important thing to consider would be the extent of the bereaved person's grief, not whether or not everybody else thinks it's fitting.

Another thing that I find trying is that people will sometimes assume that I'm upset about the death of a cat because I don't have any children. Why they should think there is a limit on the amount of love that one can have, I really do not understand. I have friends who have children, but that certainly hasn't meant that they have felt less grief over the loss of a much-loved pet. In fact, their grief has often been compounded by having to cope with the sorrow of others as well as their own.

Sometimes, of course, the cat has been a much truer friend than some human family members – but saying something like that tends to be frowned upon at best or confirm one's madness at worst!

*Allow me this unreasonable grief.*
*You say it's nothing. He was just a cat.*
*I found him dead this morning,*
*Cold where fluid warmth once flowed.*
*I loved his beauty and his selfish ways,*
*His bulky presence sprawled across the bed,*
*His casual shredding of a favourite chair.*
*I see him in the shadows everywhere,*
*And feel the snowshoe softness of his paws.*
*My grief is real. He meant the world to me.*

# DEMON KITTEN

Of course there are kittens that are perfectly capable of gracing chocolate boxes and looking the picture of innocence in the process, but I have to say that of the hundreds of kittens I have encountered, these have been very much in the minority.

Kittens, regardless of looks, are generally completely bonkers and completely fearless. A kitten who is quiet and nervous is likely to be ill or to have been traumatised by rough handling or worse. All the advice is, sensibly, to choose a kitten that is bold and playful, but that doesn't prevent most of us choosing the sad little creature with a runny nose who will cost us a fortune in vets' bills and worry us half to death. Having driven us to the brink of despair, such kittens are quite likely to suddenly pull themselves together and live into their twenties.

I've noticed that most kittens seem to concentrate initially on growing their ears and then rest on their laurels for a while until they suddenly decide to give attention to their paws, or possibly their tail. This can be quite startling for the inexperienced owner, but in the end most strange looking kittens seem to mature into perfectly normal looking cats, although sometimes the chocolate box numbers fail to fulfil their early promise – something that any plain child unfortunate enough to be in a class full of curly-haired cherubs would do well to remember.

*With a dirt tray the size of Lake Garda*
*And three tons of food in the larder,*
*You would have expected a tiger*
*To be sprawled in front of the Aga,*
*Instead of a very small kitten*
*That you could very easily tread on.*
*The baby's ears were enormous*
*And her voice unbelievably raucous;*
*She was skinny and striped like a humbug,*
*Merging only too well with the hearthrug*
*And sadly her favourite hobby*
*Was pouncing on dogs in the lobby.*
*She'd jump out and swing on their tails,*
*Sending one collie dog off the rails,*
*While another hound hid in the flowers,*
*Preferring the wind and the showers*
*To the needles attached to her paws*
*And the pins contained in her jaws.*
*Nobody has dared voiced their fears*
*That one day she'll grow into her ears.*
*If that comes to pass then a tiger*
*Will indeed be in front of the Aga.*

# TABITHA'S HERITAGE

Many years ago, I had a dear little black cat called Tabitha. I had recently moved to a safer, cat-friendly location after losing two very dear cats on a road which had become busier than any road has a right to be. I moved with just one rather clever ginger boy, Thomas, who had successfully negotiated the nightmare road for six years and was rewarded now with a large wooded garden and a plentiful supply of mice – if he could be bothered.

It had always been my plan to have more cats once I'd moved and a couple of weeks later I chose two black cats, Tabitha and Spooki, at the old Cats Protection shelter at New Malden (no longer in existence). Thomas hardly noticed their arrival and in my youthful naivety, I hadn't given a thought to how introductions should be handled. With beginner's luck, I had no problems at all and everybody settled down without so much as a fluffed-out tail.

Tabitha was a sweet tea-cosy of a cat while Spooki was a hunter, bringing me an endless supply of slugs, feathers and the occasional mouse. She branched out into 'hunting' sausages and rashers of bacon, but nobody ever mentioned anything, so I can only assume she was a rather superior type of cat burglar. Even Tabitha, however, had her wilder side and I noticed that at dusk she would shed her mild ways and slink into the garden, a wild gleam in her eyes. It was Tabitha who taught me that tea-cosies and tigers share the same heritage.

*The passing of the tiger*
*Is marked by quaking leaves,*
*By strident calls*
*And golden crescents in the night.*
*His mighty head shakes diamonds*
*From dark, deep water*
*And on he walks,*
*His strength contained*
*In soft-sprung tread.*
*His senses mock*
*Our feeble understanding of the world,*
*Scenting the fear in trembling flesh,*
*Hearing the heartbeats*
*Of a thousand frightened things*
*Where we hear silence.*
*He moves now with quiet purpose:*
*The screaming kill,*
*Inevitable and swift,*
*Heralds short-lived peace.*
*The storm has broken;*
*The moon has washed her face.*

# VET TRIP

I have a cat at the moment who actually doesn't mind going to the vet and the shock has been overwhelming!

When I had a large number of fostered cats I would make frequent journeys to have them checked over, neutered, inoculated – in fact if two days went by without me making an appointment, the vet would be quite worried. My own cats viewed this activity with expressions of exquisite boredom, but everything changed when I was limbering up to take one of them. They would look at each other and a kind of bush telegraph would come into play, with cat after cat flinging themselves at the cat flap or diving behind the sofa long before the cat carrier had made an appearance.

On numerous occasions I would have to phone and apologise because Boofuls had given me the slip/severed a main artery (mine) or was holding me at gunpoint. Rarely would we reach the end of our very short cul-de-sac without the cat chucking up or worse and even if he or she did manage to contain all bodily fluids until we entered the surgery, I could be confident that this happy state of affairs would change once the creature was hoisted on to the vet's pristine white table.

*Wherever is the wretched cat –*
*Larger than life and twice as fat?*
*As darkness falls he saunters back*
*And glares at me. I shut the flap.*
*The basket is too small, of course,*
*Compelling me to use brute force,*
*To wrestle in the twenty paws*
*That he's grown while out of doors.*
*Now we're on our way at last,*
*But I dare not drive too fast,*
*As warning noises from the rear*
*Re-awaken age-old fears;*
*He's vomited across the seat*
*And down his chest and on his feet.*
*Close to tears, I reach the vet's,*
*Carry in this dismal wretch*
*And contemplate a cat-free life,*
*Removed from vomiting and strife.*
*The vet is no more than a child –*
*No match for something quite so wild;*
*Soon the table's drenched in wee*
*(To be reflected in the fee)*
*And as she shoves the needle in,*
*Boofuls swipes her on the chin.*
*I gather up my furry bundle*
*And much poorer, homeward trundle*
*To dollop out his favourite tea*
*And pour a double gin for me.*

# THE OLD BLIND CAT

This is not meant to be a dreary poem – rather a tribute to the enduring resilience of our dear old cat, Miss Poppet, who lost her sight quite suddenly due to high blood pressure. The vet prescribed medication to bring her blood pressure down, but she was 23 years old by this stage and she hated the medication, so everybody agreed that she should live out her remaining days as peacefully and happily as possible.

Apart from seeking more physical reassurance than previously, she made no concessions to this apparently minor inconvenience and continued to enjoy lazing in the garden on sunny days, a pleasure only exceeded by her eager consumption of as many meals as she could cram down. She was a skinny old thing, her ancient insides struggling to extract sufficient nourishment from the food she stuffed down so enthusiastically.

Miss Poppet retained her feistiness to the end, revelling in her sole occupancy of one sofa while Roger and I, together with four or five cats, squeezed up on the other one. Any cat that attempted to sneak up beside her would be firmly and painfully rebuffed by a stinging slap, proving if proof were needed that Miss Poppet was still very much in charge.

*She came at suppertime with measured tread,*
*Brushed the door frame, veered over to the right,*
*But made no fuss – just wanting to be fed,*
*As if it was a trifling thing to lose her sight.*
*I held her close and stroked her old cat fur*
*And told her that her life could still be good;*
*She managed one loud, rumbling, throaty purr*
*Before demanding several plates of food.*
*On balmy days she navigates the way*
*Between the roses and wisteria bower*
*To roll in catnip, dreaming of the days*
*When she would hunt and trembling mice would cower.*
*Now she has unlimited attention*
*And doesn't anguish over wrinkles on her face;*
*She thinks that blindness isn't worth a mention,*
*Accepting growing old with feline grace.*

# EVOLUTION

When I was still working, I frequently nursed murderous thoughts as I staggered off on bitterly cold and dark winter mornings to catch the 7.30am to London if I made the mistake of glancing back at my little feline treasures reclining by the warm air vents. Not only would they not give two in the moon about their human coping with such challenges, but they would have the nerve to look irritated if a suggestion of cold air ruffled their coats as I departed.

In summer, I would watch my husband pushing the mower up and down what passes for a lawn while a tabby gazed down in wonderment from the summerhouse roof, with a disdainful look which he might have found amusing on a lazier day with a beer in his hand.

Yes – it's hard to see why we should ever have thought that we were at the top of the evolutionary tree. It's even harder to see why we're so intoxicated with these dreadful creatures!

*The tabby's asleep on the summerhouse roof*
*Beating time to her dreams with her tail;*
*She soaks up the sun while her owner, poor man,*
*Shoves the mower up hill and down dale.*
*She couldn't care less about famines and wars,*
*Doesn't worry if she should be thinner;*
*She's warming her bones in the bright summer sun*
*With the prospect of chicken for dinner.*
*So next time you think about science and such,*
*Evolution and similar matters,*
*Consider that cat – carefree and relaxed –*
*And her owner with nerves all in tatters.*

# THEY KNOW HOW TO WOUND

Presumably there are people who skip off on holiday without a backward glance, but as most of our friends are cat owners we don't know many of that carefree breed. In the days when we still had a fairly normal number of cats, we would steel ourselves to take them to the cattery, making speeches to each other about how much we needed a break and how the cats would be absolutely fine as soon as we'd left. None of this prevented us from carrying the picture with us of those sad furry faces squashed against the wire, ensuring that we spent the entire holiday feeling guilty.

Cat lovers must be incredibly slow learners, because after every holiday we would rush to collect the cats, who would either look us as if they had never seen us before or rush into their igloos with a look of abject terror – hardly the actions of cats who had spent the long days pining for their adored owners. We refused to blame them, determined to punish ourselves for their cruel behaviour.

It's not quite so bad now. With a tribe of 'special needs' cats with a plethora of problems, we – and they – are fortunate to have a very dear friend to stay with them and pander to their every whim. Leaving for the holiday is therefore rather less of an emotional rollercoaster and we sometimes depart relatively cheerfully – or at least speaking to each other.

None of this prevents us from missing them terribly, of course, and as other holidaymakers reach for the treasured photographs of their grandchildren, we will already have extracted a fistful of pictures of dear Benjamin Wobble and the rest of our furry family. We shall also be checking our mobile phones rather too frequently, eager for text messages from the long-suffering cat sitter, being convinced that an absence of communication must mean that there has been a crisis.

There is a plus to be extracted from this bizarre behaviour. As the last day of the holiday dawns and our companions are becoming drearier by the minute, we will be eagerly awaiting the reunion with Benjamin and the gang – even if they haven't realised we've been away.

*There hadn't been a moment of the day*
*When Arthur hadn't featured in our thoughts;*
*In fact it almost wrecked the holiday –*
*Even in our dreams we were distraught.*
*We grabbed the box as soon as we reached home*
*And headed for the cattery at speed;*
*We pictured Arthur waiting all alone,*
*Too desperate to play or sleep or feed.*
*I'd like to say he mewed with anguished pleasure*
*When he heard our voices drawing near;*
*Instead of which our much-loved little treasure*
*Turned his back and washed his ample rear.*

# CHRISTMAS CATS

When I was wondering what to call this book, I thought about the comfort and cosiness that cats bring into our lives (when they're not driving us mad, of course!) and never is this more in evidence in our home than at Christmas.

I don't know about you, but I've had some pretty grim Christmas days in the past – notably when I was on my own and much given to imagining everybody else having wonderfully happy times with their families while I opened a bottle of El Plonko and tried to believe that 25th December really was 'just another day'. It's ridiculous, of course. Once things returned to normal, I would be regaled with the most alarming tales about family rows, children beating each other to a pulp and disastrous festive feasts. Needless to say, none of this prevented me for feeling sorry myself all over again the following year.

Even in my darker moments, the cats were there – blithely unaware of anything other than the need to stretch out on the warm sofa, legs in the air, the occasional twitching paw and surprised chirrup the only interruptions to the sweetest of Christmas dreams.

*The shops are all shut, the gifts have been wrapped –*
*We've stocked up on wine and food for the cats;*
*Now we must wait for the magic to fall,*
*Suddenly, softly over us all.*
*We've heard the same carols for so many years,*
*Watched the old films, shed easy tears,*
*But touching a cat vibrating with purrs*
*Always makes something special occur.*
*The spirit of Christmas, of kindness and love,*
*Will just for a while flutter down from above*
*And then all the glitter, the music and lights*
*Will no longer seem tawdry, but somehow just right.*

# TABBY OR NOT TABBY?

When people came to look at cats and kittens, it always amused me to see what power could be wielded by a very small child. One such infant encountered an ancient tabby resident as they walked through the bungalow en route to the cat pens and decided that she must have Bonnie Bun-Bun, come hell or high water. It took her parents and I around half an hour to persuade the dear child that Bonnie wasn't going anywhere because I would never be able to manage without the bossy old matriarch. Eventually we progressed to the pens where kittens of every colour, shape and size could be seen leaping up the wire, while their mothers looked bored and in need of a good night out with the girls.

I realised by this stage that things were not going to be easy with 'Madam' still smarting over the Bonnie Bun-Bun episode, but hadn't bargained for her wanting the most wayward kitten in the pens, which just happened to be tabby. In vain I tried to deflect her towards a placid piebald boy; when that failed, I hoped that a sweet little tortoiseshell might win the day, but the tabby had effortlessly captured the child's affections and in so doing had rounded up the parents as well.

I am delighted to say that everything went amazingly well and in a very short time those poor parents were being bossed about not just by their rather precocious daughter, but also by an extremely precocious tabby kitten.

*Shall we have a tabby cat?*
*That's the burning question;*
*But if I might just interject*
*With a small suggestion,*
*Wouldn't cream or black and white*
*Be less rough and wild*
*And possibly less frightening*
*For the dog and for the child?*
*But even as I speak the words,*
*I'm on a hopeless mission;*
*The child, aged five, has spoken*
*And that is her decision.*
*And so we choose a tabby cat*
*With naughty tabby paws;*
*It swoops just like a furry bat*
*And opens all the doors.*
*It shreds the curtains and our nerves*
*And drives us half insane*
*But love is quite irrational –*
*We'd do the same again.*

# COMPUTER CAT

What did cats do before computers were invented? When you think how many cats have their own websites and Facebook pages, it makes you realise how frustrated they must have been, waiting for us to finish with stone tablets, work our way through parchment and clumsy old printing presses until finally we stumbled on the Internet.

At last, they thought. These slow and clumsy humans are beginning to catch up with our lightning thought processes, but only with the aid of artificial intelligence. In another few thousand years they might even be able to catch mice or see in the dark, but they will never have the mysterious powers that enable us to know what will happen before it happens, or to melt into shadows even as they gaze upon us...

Even cats that haven't aspired to their own cyberspace territory have been quick to see the advantages of sharing with us. Sometimes their interest is restricted to dabbing frenziedly at the screen in a doomed attempt to kill the cursor; sometimes, as in Tiny's case, it's a power thing which means she has to fire off my emails when she feels like it, delete things as the fancy takes her, or shut the whole system down if there's an 'r' in the month.

A further speciality is kicking over cups of coffee or, later in the day, glasses of El Plonko, necessitating prolonged hospital stays for Lenny Laptop and therapy for me.

*Softest paws upon the keys*
*Wreaking havoc with such ease,*
*Sending emails everywhere*
*With such practised feline flair,*
*Computer Cat's a playful puss –*
*Causing endless rows and fuss.*
*Favouring the asterisk*
*As across the keys she frisks,*
*She manages with frightening ease*
*To bring strong people to their knees.*
*Some suspect a dodgy virus,*
*Which, of course, is not desirous;*
*Others buy a new computer,*
*Software, hardware, modem, router.*
*Some, however, smell a rat,*
*Or even one small naughty cat.*

# THE NEW RUG

I am not remotely house-proud, but every now and then – usually when the sun is bright enough to fight its way through the lines of sneezy cat snot on the windows – I feel an urge to tart the old homestead up. Nothing fundamental, you understand – just one or two new cushion covers or, on one momentous occasion, a new rug.

I saw the rug in a sale in downtown Woking and decided there and then that it would transform not only my room, but my life. These were, of course, totally unrealistic expectations, but it had been a tough old week. The rug was amazingly heavy, but the people at the shop were determined to get it into my car – and succeeded, leaving me with a slightly obscured view of the road, which was quite a challenge when tackling the numerous roundabouts that appeared to have sprung up since I left home.

I manhandled the rug indoors and after much lifting and moving of furniture succeeded in spreading my new purchase out across the floor. The cats pretended they hadn't noticed, yawning and snoring and generally giving the impression that I would have to do something considerably more exciting than that to make it worth wrenching open their heavy eyelids.

It was a pleasant afternoon and I wandered out into the garden to cool down. I wasn't at all surprised to find that after a few minutes the cats had trailed out after me and for a short time I enjoyed a sense of achievement and well-being. Sadly, this happy state of affairs came to an abrupt end when I noticed first one cat and then several tugging at their claws and shaking their front paws in considerable agitation. I then realised that somehow tufts from the carpet had become lodged between their toes.

Bless their furry little hearts, they had obviously taken one look at the new rug and concluded that it would benefit enormously from a good raking. Sparing no effort, they had made short work of the task. How uncomfortable it must have been for those poor creatures with all those rotten old lumps of wool between their toes... and to think that I have been known to describe myself as a cat lover!

*I was so pleased with that new rug,*
*Obtained at great expense –*
*I couldn't wait to get it home*
*And feel its pile so dense.*
*I rushed to clear the cluttered room*
*Of chairs and several cats,*
*Who looked at me as if they thought*
*I'd gone completely bats.*
*The rug looked lovely on the floor –*
*A calming rural scene*
*Set off by a leafy frame*
*Of softest swirling greens.*
*I felt quite hot and bothered then,*
*So wandered off outdoors,*
*Accompanied by all my cats*
*With green tufts in their claws.*

# PARTNERS IN CRIME

No-one could ever, with any vestige of justification, accuse cats of being team players. Dogs are completely different and have only to see other dogs running about to know that the one thing that would make them happy would be to join in and run along with them. It doesn't matter where those dogs are going – it would be the most exciting thing in the world to be going with them.

Even feline litter-mates usually manage to fall out by the time they are a few months old. They might still enjoy cuddling up together, but co-operating in any structured way to achieve a particular objective is not generally high on their list of priorities.

Two of my 'special needs' cats – Whizzy, who had lost a hind leg in a road traffic accident and Stumpy Malone, who was born without hind paws – couldn't stand the sight of each other, so it was quite amusing to see them team up when Stumpy found a frog in the garden.

Over the years we have had many adventures of a froggy nature. One of the most memorable was when an extremely jolly evening gathering at Tresta Towers was interrupted by pretty little black and white Isabelle bringing in a very lively frog. I managed to catch it and disappeared into the depths of the back garden, followed closely by Isabelle who had eluded capture. I can only say that it seemed a good idea at the time to climb over the fence and place the frog in next door's pond.

Mission accomplished, I attempted to climb back, only to realise that the ground was much lower on the neighbour's side. Frustratingly, I could hear the merry laughter and tinkling of glasses issuing forth from our lounge. Eventually, I managed to grab a tree branch and haul myself back. The bad news was that nobody was the slightest bit concerned about my protracted absence from the party; the good news was that they didn't seem to notice that I burst through the patio door looking like a deranged witch from a budget version of Macbeth.

*They had never liked each other –*
*Whizzy and Malone;*
*He was so irritating,*
*Never leaving her alone.*
*But when he found a bright green frog*
*By the garden fence,*
*Whizzy thought that chumming up*
*Made a lot of sense.*
*A game of tiddlywinks ensued –*
*The height of feline fun –*
*Until I scooped old froggy up*
*And set off at the run*
*To place him safely in a pond*
*In a secret place;*
*Whizzy blamed Malone, of course,*
*And slapped him round the face.*

# RETURN TO THE WOODS

My father was firmly of the opinion that cats are takers, not givers, and if he thought this was true of cats generally, he was absolutely adamant that wild cats, or ferals, were at the extreme end of the 'taker' continuum.

I have always admired feral cats for their hardiness and sheer impudence. I found it difficult at first to understand how absolutely wild true ferals are, given that they are exactly the same genetically speaking as ordinary 'tea cosy' cats, but this is probably part of their fascination. Adult ferals are virtually impossible to tame. Even kittens of more than a few weeks old are pretty tricky and unlikely to become completely confident with people other than their immediate family.

For this reason, the normal policy of animal welfare organisations is to try and tame very young kittens so that they can be homed; adults are trapped humanely and whisked off to the vet for checking over, blood testing and neutering. The 'adjusted' feral is then returned and released. If possible, feeding is arranged; otherwise the cat or cats will fend for themselves.

Sometimes, however, there is a maniac threatening to kill the cats or the location is so perilous that efforts are made to relocate them elsewhere. Over the years I have had many feral cats and it has given me enormous pleasure to see them living out their lives in my garden. Our oldest feral currently is Spitfire – no clue in the name obviously – and she is a frosty-faced black girl, who could never be accused of showing even a hint of gratitude for the frequent meals and warm bedding we have provided for more than 15 years. She is as wild today as the day she arrived and we love her for it.

Inevitably, having feral cats brings its share of heartaches as they are much given to disappearing when they feel the end is near. Even if we've realised they are ill, catching them is a considerable challenge and could cause terrible stress to what is essentially a wild animal. Hard though it is, the kindest option is usually to let these wonderful cats do what wild animals do and return to the wild.

*'She looks the same,' they say,*
*'as any other cat.' They do not know*
*that she has come from the woods*
*and hears wild music*
*in the wind that chases clouds*
*across the craters of the moon.*
*She will catch and eat a slow, fat pigeon*
*before its heart stops beating*
*and turn to glare at you,*
*with blood and feathers on her lips,*
*daring you to be disgusted*
*and caring less than nothing if you are.*
*She is beautifully black,*
*plump as a plum with a milky sheen*
*because she condescends to eat*
*expensive cat food, hunched over bowls*
*that the fox will steal during the night*
*and dump in ferny caverns.*
*She is contemptuous of us,*
*offended by our sentimental ways;*
*in the end she will reject us*
*and return to the undemanding woods.*

# PHARAOH AND FLUFFY

Most of our cats are not 'proper' cats and consequently we are largely untroubled by mice being deposited in various corners of our bijou residence. Evie, however, frequently arrives at the patio door with an impressive mouse moustache. This is not universally welcomed – by us or by the other feline residents.

Such negative reactions must be very confusing for the likes of Evie, since cats were originally domesticated for their rodent-catching prowess and to have some silly woman screaming and trying to rescue the mouse that they've just spent a lot of time and effort catching must seem extremely ungrateful if not downright rude.

Although Evie is a competent mouser, she still has a long way to go to compete with a cat I had years ago who counted it a failure if she hadn't despatched half a dozen mice by lunch time. Not only did this dedicated huntress sort out the mice, she also kept the local grass snakes on their toes, as it were, by dragging them through the cat flap and giving them a tour of the kitchen. They were always unharmed and enjoyed lurking under the cooker, emerging as I cooked the evening meal. The first time this happened, I must admit to a slight overreaction, but I soon pulled myself together and made sure that for future incidents I had an empty bread bin handy to transport Sammy Snake back to the woods.

*The mighty Pharaoh cursed and sighed*
*As he beheld the shrivelled grain;*
*His beaten slaves were terrified*
*And begged their numerous gods for rain.*

*At last one day a steady drizzle*
*Made the desert green and lush;*
*Without their daily dose of sizzle*
*The ancient pyramids turned to rust.*
*The sun came back to do its duty,*
*Ears of corn grew gold and fat*
*And while he smiled to see such beauty,*
*Old Pharaoh thought he smelt a rat.*
*Soon the sneaky, greedy creature*
*Saw its chance to grab a snack.*
*In fact the rat became a feature*
*Rummaging amongst the sacks.*
*In no time a rodent army*
*Thrived within the granary store,*
*Driving desperate Pharaoh barmy*
*And leaving husks upon the floor.*
*Luckily, a cat called Fluffy*
*Heard about the Pharaoh's plight;*
*Off she flew – a feline toughie –*
*And had it sorted overnight.*
*As the grateful Pharaoh, Ramesses,*
*Stroked her rather tattered ears,*
*Fluffy knew that her relations*
*Would be worshipped through the years.*

# THERE'S MORE TO LIFE

I'm rather inclined to make bracing speeches from time to time – usually to myself, which is probably just as well. I know this will surprise you, but a lot of my speeches relate to being made a total fool of by cats and resolving not to let it happen again.

The great consolation is that at any time of day or night there are millions of other cat lovers waiting for ungrateful felines to manifest themselves at doors and windows across the globe and every one of them is alternating between incandescent rage and desperate worry. When the wretched creature arrives, the initial relief is, of course, overwhelming, but it doesn't take long for feelings of resentment to creep in. What right have these cats to treat us like this? It's not a lot to ask, is it? Then the guilt, until finally you're an emotional wreck and wondering why anybody has ever described cats as a calming influence.

Then there's the food. We have recently adopted a 16 year old cat, Harriet-Smudge, who had previously been an only cat and therefore found it quite a challenge to settle down with this happy band of moggy misfits. We were desperate to get her to eat properly and spent a fortune on providing a luxurious running buffet in an attempt to bring a smile to that anxious little grumpy face. How foolish! Eventually I tried her on bog-standard supermarket cat food and Harriet fell upon it, pausing only to fling a reproachful look in my direction.

Of course, we have all experienced situations where a furry life has hung by a thread and if you thought that caviar would work the miracle you would take out another mortgage and fill every shelf in the fridge with the stuff. At such desperate times there is a tendency to smack the well-meaning person who suggests that thinking about global warming and the economic situation would help you to get things in perspective. If the same person were to appear when a corner has been turned you would clasp her to your bosom and invite her to come on holiday with you. But there are other occasions when Boofuls and friends definitely push their luck and this silly rhyme is dedicated to them.

*I never, ever would allow a cat to call the shots;*
*Like dogs and tricky children, he needs to know I'm boss.*
*I'd never be a sad old sack, staying up all night,*
*Or searching for expensive things to tempt his appetite.*
*A cat's a cat, I've always said – a pleasant pet it's true,*
*But as for being that cat's slave – I've better things to do!*
*I might well take a holiday; I wouldn't hesitate,*
*But sadly now I've left the booking up too late;*
*I'd never think of waiting up until he wandered home;*
*After all, I know too well that cats were born to roam.*
*I've always said to anxious friends, 'He's just a half-wild creature;*
*I wasn't waiting up for him – I watched a special feature.'*
*Today I bought some toys and spent a fortune on the cat –*
*I'm glad I'm not a slave to him – there's more to life than that.*

# JELLICLE CATS AND THEIR FRIENDS

There is comfort to be found in remembering the clever and famous people that have loved cats, particularly when people are looking at you as if you've got two heads just because you've bought a bed for Fluffy that cost more than your car did.

I took a phone call from a cat magazine while I was working in an open plan office and was so excited when they told me I'd won a competition that I quite forgot where I was.

'Oh!' I exclaimed, 'I'm so thrilled! I never dared to hope that I might actually win!'

I think I carried on in this vein for some time and obviously quite loudly, because by the time I replaced the receiver the other girls were looking at me strangely.

'Well – come on, tell us! What have you won?'

'A year's supply of cat food!' I squeaked, 'and a big rosette!'

'What was the competition?' my colleagues asked nervously.

I was bursting with pride. 'It's Tabitha,' I explained. 'She's won the Glamorous Granny competition at Cat World.'

Now, I'm not suggesting for a moment that this puts me – or Tabitha – in the same league as that cat-loving poet, dear Mr T S Eliot, but I cling to the hope that he would at least understand. And I'm sure he would have enjoyed looking at Tabitha's rosette, which I came across the other day and relived the euphoria of that distant afternoon.

*That nice Mr Eliot wrote about cats*
*And Jellicle cats in particular;*
*Andrew Lloyd Webber's musical, Cats,*
*Featured their tails perpendicular.*
*A Jellicle cat should be black and white,*
*Dressed, as it were, for fine dining;*
*His shirt is always startlingly bright,*
*His cufflinks distinguished and shining.*
*Some of his friends reside down the road –*
*You have possibly heard of a few –*
*Spellicle lives with a witch and a toad,*
*Smellicle makes quite a poo;*
*Dwellicle says life indoors is for her*
*And Tellicle tells many tales;*
*Shellicle cat has tortoiseshell fur*
*And Cellicle's banged up in jail.*
*Wellicle cat sports long rubber boots;*
*And Bellicle's feeding his tummy;*
*Some say way back in the Rellicle roots*
*There once was a cat that had money.*
*So when a feline you happen to see*
*In the street, or perhaps down the pub,*
*Just be aware it could easily be*
*A member of that elite club.*

# A TIGER IN THE AVENUE

Years ago, Roger and I travelled into Hertfordshire to visit a leopard sanctuary. As we pottered down a respectable suburban street, we became convinced that we had taken a wrong turning and even when the road name and house number matched what we were looking for, we were half expecting someone to jump out and tell us we were on some silly reality show.

Behind this perfectly normal looking house there were extensive fields, with enormous pens where a selection of feline beauties reclined and growled – when they could be bothered or felt it was expected. The occasion was an open day for photographers and Roger was soon snapping away with the best of them, while I drooled over the animals and hoped nobody would be too jealous of my Kodak Brownie.

It was a magical day and just when I thought things couldn't get much better, the owner of the sanctuary brought a young leopard along on a lead. He had been hand-reared because his mother didn't have enough milk for him, and he was great friends with the owner's German Shepherd dog. I stroked him and noticed how interested he was in scenting my handbag – an interest reciprocated by my own cats who must have had nightmares about where we'd been that wonderful afternoon.

It was that excursion that made me think how amusing it would be to have a big cat living in an ordinary house and how it would give some nosy neighbours something apart from badly parked cars and fallen leaves to worry about.

*I wish I had a tiger with stripes and massive paws*
*To sit upon the windowsill while nibbling at his claws.*
*He'd frighten the poor postman and make him drop the mail*
*And always make a dreadful draught swishing that long tail.*
*The cats along the avenue are boring and demure –*
*Playing with their catnip mice and smoothing down their fur,*
*But if I had a tiger he'd make them catch their breath*
*And if their owners saw him it would scare them half to death.*
*I'd call my tiger 'Tiddles' and take him out to play,*
*Scaring all the people and chasing dogs away.*
*He'd run and kick a football and often even score,*
*Leaving players claiming that Tiddles broke the law,*
*Because he hadn't paid his subs and didn't have a shirt,*
*But Tiddles would just laugh at them and piddle in the dirt.*
*It would shake up that dull avenue which wouldn't be so twee*
*If Tiddles came to live with me at number twenty-three.*

# A BOY NAMED DAISY

Deciding whether a kitten is male or female isn't easy and even seasoned kitten handlers have been known to get things wrong – and that certainly includes me. A very fluffy bottom can present a particular challenge and a wriggling kitten is tricky enough to hang on to without the added problem of getting a good look at its rear end trimmings through smeary varifocals.

A dear friend of mine decided some years ago that she would like a kitten and, as is the way of things, another friend of hers duly arrived with a perky little black and white number who was christened 'Daisy'. People often experience feelings of shock when visiting the vet, but on this occasion it wasn't just the bill that floored my friend – it was the discovery that little Daisy was in fact a boy.

Most people would have renamed the kitten, but to my friend's eternal credit she stuck to her guns, explaining that she had always liked the name and the kitten was used to it. Now, in my experience, most cats don't care too much about their name and renaming the kitten 'Dave' would probably not have resulted in a need for counselling. I think cats have their own ideas about names and probably think of themselves as 'Brighter-Than-Any-Human' or 'Best-At-Losing-Expensive-Collars' rather than 'Sooty' or 'Montgomery'. And any cat that has decided to ignore a human will carry on ignoring them whatever name they're calling him or her.

Anyway, Daisy is still Daisy all these years later and brings his owner a steady supply of mice which she duly gathers up in a humane mouse trap and returns to the great outdoors. Daisy is a big cat by any standard and quite macho looking, give or take a slightly unnerving grin when overdosing on catnip. I have often thought that a vet's life probably affords few opportunities for amusement, so I'm sure being presented from time to time with a butch-looking boy cat called Daisy provides some much-needed light relief.

*You've heard of that poor boy named Sue,*
*Who didn't know quite what to do*
*When he finally met the man*
*Who should have called him Jake or Sam;*
*But what about the handsome tom*
*Who was called Daisy – what went wrong?*
*The truth was that his doting mum*
*Was quite vague about cat bums*
*And thought the kitten was a girl*
*Because 'her' tail was tightly curled.*
*The vet in due course disabused*
*The woman who was so confused;*
*She tried quite hard to change his name*
*To something that might sound the same,*
*But Davy didn't seem to fit*
*And Daisy didn't care a bit.*

# MOVING ON

I remember leaving home on this particular day in some trepidation, not helped by the insistent yowling coming from the back seat. The main cause of my uneasiness was the prospect of finding a parking space in Surbiton where my companion – a black short-haired cat – would be taking up residence. This sweet female cat had been homed by me once, only to be returned because the owner had found she was allergic to her new pet.

We reached our destination with only a few nervous breakdowns on my part and I was relieved to find that the house had its own driveway. As I turned in, tall, electronically-controlled gates swung open to reveal an imposing house in extensive grounds.

A pleasant-looking woman appeared and ushered me towards a patio table loaded with cakes and coffee cups.

'I thought you could probably do with a cuppa after fighting your way through the traffic,' she said. 'We can let the new arrival settle for a minute while you get your breath back, then we'll take her to her room.'

Within seconds, the empty patio chairs were occupied by various Persian cats, who stared at me balefully. The most baleful of all was a soft grey character with huge round amber eyes. He was introduced as Pangbourne.

'Your husband must be a cat-lover too,' I remarked clumsily.

'Not really. In fact, he said some really spiteful things to Pangbourne and then had the nerve to tell me that I had to decide between him and the cats. Well, obviously there was no contest. I can't imagine what made him think that was a sensible thing to say!'

As she spoke she extended a well-manicured hand to stroke Pangbourne's plushy coat. It's hard to describe the expression on that big flat face, but 'smug' probably comes closest. I did wonder what the poor man might have said to Pangbourne. Perhaps he called him 'Pug Face' or 'Popeye'; one thing is certain – he won't be doing it again.

*Her husband said, 'Enough's enough,*
*It's me or them, my Darling.*
*These cats have taken all your love*
*And where's the meal? I'm starving!'*
*She looked up sadly, shook her head*
*And trifled with a yawn.*
*'Where will you go?' at last she said,*
*'When you have mown the lawn?'*
*The cats watched from the windowsill*
*As Daddy slowly stumbled*
*Towards the waiting taxi cab,*
*His shirt un-ironed and crumpled.*
*So now the cats have claimed the bed*
*And everything's fur-coated.*
*You should have realised, Daddy dear,*
*That you would be out-voted.*

# A CAT FOR ALL SEASONS

A fascinating thing about cats is that you've no sooner decided that cats are ideally suited to the cosiness of winter evenings, than the clocks have jumped forward and our feline friends are skipping through the daffodils – and doing it rather well, only pausing to nip off the heads of the yellow things that so spoil the appearance of these joyous flowers.

Then we're into summer, and how anybody can think of having a garden seat without a cat snoozing away the hours is quite beyond me. Cats do justice to summer days effortlessly – this can, of course, be slightly irritating when one is sweating buckets in a futile effort to knock the garden into shape under the bored gaze of a sun-soaked cat.

Autumn frequently whisks in with buffeting winds which see the most staid of cats flattening their ears, looping their tails and doing ridiculous, stiff-legged leaps across the lawn. Exhausted by these antics, they will then come indoors and provide the perfect excuse for turning on the heating as they huddle by radiators, air vents or empty fireplace.

Then, before anybody has fully recovered from the previous Christmas, here we go again with dusting off the decorations, arguing over the relative merits of sprouts and parsnips and worrying about presents. Children and grandchildren are easily dealt with – a couple of oranges, a lecture on how tough things used to be and by the time you've finished they're just grateful to go and play outside in the freezing rain.

What really exercises the mind is what to buy for the cats in your life; would a bumper pack of Kittydins Special Treats be acceptable, or does that show a lack of imagination? What about that game where Tiddles has to extract yummy things from a scary plastic creation with various strangely-shaped cavities? Come to think of it, she had one last year from a well-meaning friend and smashed it within minutes. Never mind – it'll soon be spring.

*SPRINGTIME CAT*

*He steps into the scented garden,*
*Sniffing the freshness;*
*His owl eyes track the birds,*
*Busy in branches of dotted green.*

*SUMMER CAT*

*He stretches in pooled sunlight,*
*Kneading the warm grass,*
*One ear swivelling to catch*
*The song of shimmering wings.*

*AUTUMN CAT*

*He chases swirling leaves,*
*Wild-eyed, hook-tailed,*
*Dabbing at ghostly toadstools*
*In deserted, dappled woods.*

*WINTER CAT*

*He comes at night with frosted fur,*
*Trailing soft coldness*
*Across smooth satin pillows*
*And his owner sleeps more soundly.*

# MALCOLM, GENTLY DISAPPROVING

I had hit one of those tricky patches in my life when things were not going as I would have wished. We all have them – people you love pass on or away, houses suddenly demand drastic repairs; there are any number of things that happen in life and these challenges seem to favour the cluster approach, so that you don't have a chance to recover from one thing before another problem comes looming out of the mist to sock you in the chops.

I was feeling pretty sorry for myself when an elderly gentleman phoned Cats Protection on a chilly November evening to ask if a funny old cat he'd found in his garden could be taken in for re-homing. I said we were full at the moment, but I would put the cat on the waiting list and take him into the rescue pens as soon as there was a space. The man phoned again the next day and said he was getting quite worried about the cat, because he didn't seem to be able to eat.

An hour later, I was looking at a large bag of bones covered – more or less – in tatty, brownish-grey fur. The cat had a broken jaw, which would explain the problems with eating, and his paws were raw and bleeding. I asked the gentleman if he had given the cat a name. 'Lucky – I call him Lucky'. I managed a feeble smile and settled Lucky into the spare room.

In due course, with a wired-up jaw and paws cleaned and dressed, Lucky ate his way back to health and became a stunning cat. His moth-eaten coat was replaced by a smooth, silvery grey pelt that you could almost see your face in. Of course I kept him and, although I suppose he had been lucky in the end, I changed his name to Malcolm.

Malcolm was a wonderful companion and my special boy. Even people who professed to hate cats loved him and when he reached the end of his very long road, there was widespread mourning. By that time, I had remarried and life was good, but I will never forget the part that dear old Malcolm played in my life. I was the lucky one.

*He arrived unannounced as a battered old stray*
*And began to take over the very same day.*
*He could show disapproval by twitching his nose,*
*And the softest of mews kept me on my toes.*
*If supper was late or not up to the mark,*
*He would grunt, turn his back and head for the park*
*To commune with his chums about human failures*
*While digging up pansies and nibbling the dahlias.*
*At the end of his life, with a world weary sigh,*
*He regarded me kindly through bleary old eyes;*
*Every twitch an expression of benevolent sorrow*
*And the lingering hope I'd do better tomorrow.*

# CREMATORIUM CAT

We all know about 'horses for courses', but there are also cats that are ideally suited to a particular role in life.

Many of the cats that I've shared my life with have been allocated 'pretend' jobs, simply because something about their demeanour and character has reminded me of a person that had a certain occupation. My wonderful black and white Sammy would definitely have been a stationery clerk. He was a sweet, tidy, placid cat, who liked his meals to be served on time, on the same plate and chicken Felix would do very nicely, thank you. The last thing that dear old Sammy craved was excitement and I'm sure that he would have taken early retirement when those new-fangled computers were brought in

Ginger Charlie would definitely have been a career soldier. He was a strict disciplinarian and wouldn't take any lip from younger cats. And he was brave; he lost his sight at the age of 23, but still insisted on going into the back garden and giving those upstart foxes a run for their money. He would lash out with a skinny ginger paw and the fox would slink away, not wishing to tangle with the feline equivalent of a World War Two veteran.

Some cats though have real jobs. My own Tiny Trixie-Tribble takes her Pets as Therapy work extremely seriously and the cat that I've written about in the next poem was certainly born to be a Crematorium cat. He was a black stray that appeared in the grounds of the local Crem and just stayed. No owner was ever traced, but Solly was adopted by the very caring people who worked there and wanted for nothing. In return, this remarkable cat became a local legend and gave comfort to thousands of mourners over the years. Bless his undemanding and generous soul – the human race could learn a lot about love and empathy from dear old Solly.

*Black Solly was born with a very old face;*
*As a kitten his features were quite out of place –*
*Crumpled, scrunched up and really too serious,*
*Making him look rather stern and imperious.*

*He was dirt-tray proficient ahead of the bunch,*
*Washing his paws before eating lunch*
*And sighing as siblings chased feathers and paper;*
*Life wasn't a game – they'd realise that later!*

*The years hurried by and he fell on hard times,*
*But instead of plummeting down into crime*
*He decided to seek a respectable job,*
*Refusing to join the layabout mob.*

*The Crem at the time was seeking a cat*
*Of impeccable character, preferably black.*
*They very much liked Solly's thoughtful demeanour*
*And noticed his paws could not have been cleaner.*

*Soon he was part of every procession,*
*With a tread slow and solemn to match his expression.*
*And soon it became indisputable fact*
*That it wasn't a funeral without Solly cat.*

# MISS MARMITE

Miss Marmite belongs to some very dear friends. She is engaged to be married to my own sweet Benjamin Wobble. It is likely to be a very long engagement and this suits everybody.

The Miss Marmite of today is nothing like the original model, which was scrawny, starving and unsatisfactory in every way. What the original model possessed in spades, however, was an unshakable conviction that she was destined for better things and wasted no time in targeting a vulnerable human to assist her in turning the thought into reality.

Each day she would wait for this pleasant young man to appear. Nobody with any sense would want to waste piteous mewing on thin air, so Marmite would save it all up until she saw him. She would then fling herself into his path and give it her all, making sure that he had to pick her up so that he could feel her little sparrow bones under the dull, woolly fur.

Some people might have thought that this was all a bit of a nuisance, but this nice young man felt privileged that the kitten trusted him and worried if she failed to appear. One day, the kitten seemed quieter than usual and her hero wondered if she was unwell. He knocked on doors, but nobody seemed to know who the kitten belonged to and they certainly didn't care.

The kind young man couldn't leave the kitten to its fate. Too many people had already walked away from this vulnerable little creature, so by a circuitous route this lucky baby ended up with my lovely friends to lead the life she always knew was waiting for her – somewhere, sometime.

As is the way with cats, when the good times come they are reluctant to discuss their humble beginnings and when your coat shines like satin and you are engaged to a handsome ginger cat, why ever would you want to?

*She's the colour of Marmite –*
*A velvety black;*
*You could spread her on toast*
*When the sun's on her back.*
*She rolls in the road*
*Causing great consternation*
*And gives drivers and cyclists*
*Dire palpitations.*
*She favours a rooftop*
*And then can't get down*
*Like a jar on a shelf*
*She wobbles around*
*And then when you grab her*
*She leaps to the ground*
*And shoots down a crevice*
*In one agile bound.*
*Miss Marmite's quite nifty*
*At biffing and such*
*If someone's behaviour*
*Is just a bit much;*
*She holds definite views*
*On mealtimes and food*
*And on occasions*
*Can almost be rude.*
*But none of this matters*
*Because like the spread*
*She's the ideal companion*
*For breakfast in bed.*

# DILLON WANTS A KITTEN

In the world of animal rescue, there are many things that can challenge the fortitude of the rescuer. There are the obvious problems, like dealing with sick or frightened animals and the emotionally draining episodes that involve taking in a much-loved pet that can no longer be coped with by an elderly owner; there are also situations that make the rescuer's blood boil and call for reserves of patience rarely granted to any human being.

I suppose I'm referring to people being silly, but the implications of this for vulnerable animals are much more threatening than that innocent-sounding word suggests. During the 30 years or so that I was involved in hands-on cat rescue and re-homing, I had a fair sprinkling of 90 year old ladies who thought it would be jolly to take on a tiny kitten – presumably so they could fall over it and break their hips, but these were easily dealt with. Much trickier were the mums, sometimes living in tower blocks, who thought it would be a wonderful thing for their son or daughter to have a kitten – probably because their friend had just been given one and was having a lovely time dragging the poor thing round by the neck.

The initial phone call would be enough to strike fear in my heart as the conversation would often be conducted against a cacophony of childish screaming and alarming crashes and bangs. Often the request to come and look at kittens could be nipped in the bud by ascertaining the age of the youngest child and saying it was against our policy to home kittens with very young children; if the caller lived in a flat with no access to a garden, again the request could be turned down without the need to address more sensitive considerations.

Sometimes, however, the family would come to see the kittens and after twenty seconds of the children thumping the living daylights out of each other, I was forced to meet the challenge head-on and refuse to home a kitten with them. This did not always make me popular – in fact, some of the phrases used showed an inventive turn of mind – and, of course, I couldn't stop them getting a kitten from a pet shop or from the dreaded internet. I only wished I could.

*I'm sure he is a lovely boy,*
*But a kitten, dear, is not a toy*
*And watching as he smacks his brother*
*Makes me think he could be bother.*
*I know you'll think I'm harsh and smug,*
*But what about a pickled slug?*

# THAT DIRE DISEASE

It seems to be acceptable to have dogs. In fact, it is almost a badge of respectability as in, 'She's okay. No really, I've seen her go by with her dog.'

I offer this as a useful character reference for any reader contemplating a bank robbery or even a murder. Get yourself a dog – probably a spaniel or something suitably soft looking; a pit bull terrier could be a problem when it comes to creating the right image – and you'll almost certainly get away with it.

The thinking seems to be that if a dog thinks you're wonderful, then you obviously are. This is absolutely not true! Think of Bill Sykes and Bull's Eye – that poor dog was beaten to within an inch of its wretched life and still thought his master was the best thing ever – tinned dog food not being on the agenda at that time.

Anybody can love a creature who thinks they are the centre of the universe. It takes grit and determination to love a miserable old tortoiseshell who clearly feels deeply contemptuous about your every action and utterance. Even so, the general view of people who love cats is that they are suffering from a condition bordering on a disease. In fact the owner of several cats is likely to be perceived as a rather sad human who has had to make do because he or she was not fortunate enough to have children. This is nonsense! I would only have considered having children if for some dreadful reason I had been unable to have cats.

Even though I have been aware of this for years, I was slightly surprised (and considerably amused) when I heard that my boss had expressed amazement when she heard that I was planning to get married. Her reaction was a particularly heartwarming one.

'Heather! Getting married! But she's got cats.'

At the time of writing there is still no known cure for this most debilitating disease. And that's fine by me.

*Is she having treatment,*
*Or a minor operation?*
*Do they think it's terminal,*
*Or caused by constipation?*
*Can you tell by looking*
*At her eyes or at her lips?*
*Does she need replacement*
*Of one or both her hips?*
*Is it psychological*
*And impossible to treat?*
*Does she see it as a problem,*
*Or blame it on the heat?*
*I don't know how to tell you –*
*It is even worse than that;*
*There is no cure or treatment –*
*The poor soul has got cats!*

# THE RESIDENTS' LOUNGE

I love old cats. Even with the inevitable heartache that comes when you lose a dear old friend, I and many others would have missed out on a great deal of love and laughter if we had not accompanied them over those final furlongs.

Of course, it's silly to see them in human terms, but as far as I'm aware it isn't against the law and it is almost impossible to resist the temptation. The following poem tries to capture some of the characters who have graced my life. God rest their furry, loving little souls. And even their cantankerous, ungrateful ones!

*Nobody sits on the Colonel's chair*
*Though a great many years have flown*
*Since his skinny old body marched away*
*To the heavenly soldiers' home.*
*His grumpy, growling ghost remains*
*In the corner by the door;*
*There's ginger fur on the Colonel's chair*
*And threads pulled by his claws.*

*Today a fuzzy Persian cat*
*Reclines on a couch and snores;*
*She has more than a touch of dementia*
*And isn't allowed out of doors.*
*She has delusions of grandeur*
*And has royal blood, so she claims;*
*But none of that helps her remember*
*Even one of her pedigree names.*

*A fragile and faded tortoiseshell*
*Will occasionally condescend*

*To stagger across the Residents' Lounge,*
*When seeking an ear to bend.*
*She reminisces monotonously*
*About fame on the London stage*
*While the rest of the ancient residents*
*Dribble with impotent rage.*

*Sometimes there'll be a concert*
*When a frail Siamese comes to play;*
*She plonks away in a heavy-pawed way*
*And it seems to go on for days.*
*Most of the cats just warble along,*
*But not so old Tabby Tom,*
*Who always has to make a big scene*
*And tell her where she's going wrong.*

*On fine days there might be an outing*
*To the country or even the sea*
*And on the way home they'll remember*
*How wonderful things used to be;*
*What fun they would have as young kittens,*
*Chasing their tails in the sun,*
*How summers were endless and joyful*
*When they were all spritely and young.*

*But nobody sits in the Colonel's seat*
*At the front of the rusty old bus,*
*Or mentions how much they miss the old chap,*
*Or complains about all the fuss*
*He would make about the young driver's fur*
*Needing a good brush and a comb*
*Because he might be watching them still*
*From the heavenly soldiers' home.*

# SPOOKS AND PICKLE

Picture, if you will, two country cats who live in an idyllic location with every opportunity to pursue their sporting interests. These cats take their rightful place in the grand scheme of things: their owners are quite happy to see them frisking about outside and will even put down the odd plate of food on a fairly random basis, but the cats are certainly not at the top of their agenda.

When they move away, there isn't a thought in the owners' heads about taking the cats with them. The cats, quite simply, go with the house, so off the owners go, leaving behind two slightly puzzled cats. The fact that the new owner isn't scheduled to move in for a while is just one of those things.

Fortunately for Spooks and Pickle, the new owner saw things rather differently and when she heard that these poor cats had been abandoned, she took immediate action to secure their wellbeing, while recognising that these were two independent, healthy cats – not the sort of couch potatoes that some of us share our lives with.

Fast forward a few months. Could this be Pickle, sprawled across her owner's bed? Could this be Spooks, sleeping soundly on the leather office chair while his owner crouches uncomfortably on a stool, attempting to view the computer screen through a blur of black and white fur?

Could this be the sensible person who took such a matter-of-fact view of cat ownership just a short time ago, now scouring supermarket shelves for new and exciting flavours of cat food? And worrying about injured paws and possible referrals to specialists? And celebrating wildly when the invalid returns to rude health?

Yes.

*He is handsome, dressed for dinner,*
*Black and white and very sweet.*
*Pickle's tortie, sharp and feisty,*
*Quick as crotchets on her feet.*
*Forgotten are the chilly evenings,*
*Spent in sad and draughty sheds;*
*Spooks and Pickle condescend now*
*To stretch out on comfy beds.*
*Their owner's efforts to engage them*
*In the cultural side of life*
*Have proved largely unsuccessful –*
*They still prefer to play with mice.*
*In the lean times they would wolf down*
*Gristly meat and dubious fish,*
*But now they toy with gourmet platters,*
*Served promptly on a fancy dish.*
*Are they grateful? Gentle reader,*
*If with cats you've ever lived*
*You will know that feline gratitude*
*Is like water in a sieve.*

# FLUFFY'S DOWNFALL

I often think that cat owners derive almost as much pleasure from catnip as their cats. It's one tough cookie who can watch a cat rolling on its back, legs in the air, oblivious to everything, without giggling – and I'm as guilty as the next person, although I always tried to spare the cat's feelings, naturally.

In the same way as there is something particularly amusing about a stiff and starchy person getting tipsy or doing something daft, it's always funny when a rather self-possessed or prim sort of cat indulges in a catnip trip.

On summer days I often sprinkled dried catnip on the back lawn as a treat for the various ferals who have lived with us over the years. Young Tufty would watch the others rolling around with an expression of contempt twitching on those glistening black lips, but once they had all lurched away to recover their composure, he would stride across the lawn. As the irresistible smell assailed his nostrils, he would glance furtively to left and right, then flop down and wriggle on the warm grass, coating his gleaming fur with catnip dust. After a few moments he would leap to his feet and stride away, with only a few green streaks across his bottom to give the game away.

Our old tortoiseshell, Joan Collins, could be slow to see the joke, but after a few whiffs of catnip she was well away. Joan lived to a great age and in her mid-twenties often needed to be helped up after a particularly vigorous session – and I am still talking about catnip and about the cat!

*Every so often the BBC News*
*Features a tale dark and sinister.*
*When you read on, you won't be surprised,*
*That this one brought down several Ministers.*
*Young Fluffy had seemed such an innocent cat,*
*A home-loving, warm-natured girl,*
*Until Auntie Gladys gave her a toy –*
*A mouse knitted in plain and in purl.*
*Contained in this mouse, it pains me to say,*
*Were the seeds of the poor cat's downfall;*
*She succumbed to the lure of pungent catnip*
*And was found outside having a ball.*
*Rolling around with her legs in the air,*
*Without a thought so it seems*
*For her owners, the neighbours, the postman and all*
*While she relished those drug-induced dreams.*
*The police backed away. 'Too dangerous,' they cried,*
*'Give us a murderer or two!*
*She's out of her mind – just look at her eyes –*
*And her language has turned the air blue!'*
*Then the tom from next door arrived unannounced*
*And distinguished himself, I must say,*
*By smacking poor Fluffy right round the chops*
*And whipping the catnip away.*

# MEDICATION

If I had a suspicious turn of mind, I would think that the manufacturers of medication for cats had a vested interest in a significant percentage of the product being wasted. Show me the person who has successfully administered a course of antibiotic tablets the size of gobstoppers to their cat and I will eat a packet of worm tablets washed down with a bottle of laxative, then take up residence in the nearest bathroom.

Vets start off with an advantage because in the pristine, brightly lit surgery, Fluffy and Gnasher will feel vulnerable. Not only is it an unfamiliar environment, but they will be worried about how they look in the unforgiving spotlight. Fluffy will wonder if the subtle grey lowlights around her ears are spreading to the point of joining up while Gnasher is likely to be preoccupied with that broken canine tooth that hasn't so far been observed in the foggy light of the standard lamp which has been a feature of home life since the main light bulb burnt out and welded itself to the fitting. Against this background of feline angst a child of three could ram a pill down and make it look easy.

At home, with their confidence restored, Fluffy and Gnasher will present a more challenging set of teeth to the world. Any feelings of inadequacy will be so far behind them as to be totally eradicated; add to this their absolute conviction that their owner is a complete idiot and you don't stand a chance. Some of my worst experiences have followed a previous triumph.

'I've cracked it now! Fluffy didn't see it coming. It's all a question of co-ordination.'

If you ever catch yourself saying things like this, be sure that you can get to A and E around the time that Fluffy's next dose is due, because cats are so good at revenge they make Nemesis look like the goddess of forgiveness.

The vet advised me – with no sign of a smile – to insert my fingers between the gap in Tiny's teeth. Hello? There is no gap! Even cats with no teeth can grow phantom teeth in an instant and come close to severing a finger. Until I had cats, I suffered under the delusion that there is a solution for every problem if only we could find it. There isn't.

*Our sofa is immune, I'm sure,*
*To sneezes, coughs and much more;*
*Our carpet never will have worms*
*Or anything at all that squirms.*

*How do I know? You may well ask,*
*But my experience is vast;*
*For every pill that Gnasher takes*
*A good half dozen go to waste.*

*Later and congealed in slime,*
*Those tablets will turn up in time*
*To stick to trousers, skirts and frocks*
*Or decorate a visitor's sock.*

# SABOTAGE

I have never aspired to being a domestic goddess, but just every now and then I would like to dish up a meal that I didn't have to apologise for. The only other way of coping with having people round is to make sure they've had plenty to drink before they sit down at the table. The longer you can leave things before serving, the more satisfactory the results will be. Not only will they be quite drunk, but they are also likely to be ravenously hungry and unlikely to quibble about lumps of cat fur, teeth marks or cats sleeping on placemats. It goes without saying that subdued lighting is a useful adjunct and a few strategically placed diffusers won't do any harm in case Fluffy's ill-gotten spoils might have upset her delicate digestive system.

If, after taking every precaution, guests do quibble, the answer is to retire to the kitchen yourself and down a bottle of El Plonko. This won't solve the problem, but at least you won't care.

However, there is great comfort to be had from the wonderful ready meals so thoughtfully provided by the likes of dear M and S and I for one won't have a word said against them. The people who risk coming here are without exception wonderful friends who are besotted with our furry companions – although possibly not quite so besotted with furry trifles. Add to this their amazement and gratitude if anything remotely edible appears in front of them before 10 o'clock at night and you will realise that a few telltale cartons and pinging microwaves really aren't the end of the world. I still wouldn't mind looking like Nigella though...

*I blame that ginger Jellytots*
*Who hatches out the darkest plots*
*While purring like a rusty motor*
*And posing for a family photo.*
*Unless I'm very much mistaken,*
*After stealing lumps of bacon,*
*He's sabotaged the peach pavlova –*
*I really don't know why I bother!*
*When the wreck I first inspected*
*I thought it might be resurrected,*
*But as I poked the shattered pud*
*I knew it didn't look too good*
*So in the end I dumped the mess*
*And legged it down to M and S.*

# THE LONGBONES

My life has been spent with moggies, so I am a total stranger to the world of pedigree cats. The very limited experience I have has been with two sweet, but extremely challenged, rescued Persians and Miss Tiny Trixie-Tribble, who was found wandering the streets of Sidcup, but has delusions of grandeur as she has a passing resemblance to a Bengal. She has unfortunately been encouraged in this misapprehension by well-meaning people who have told her how beautiful she is and how much she reminds them of Bengal cats they have seen at various cat shows.

A very dear friend of ours who loves all cats has a particular fondness for Orientals. On first being introduced to these elegant creatures, I was struck by the length of their bodies and limbs, surrounded as I am at home by rather porky bodies supported by stubby little legs. I thought of them immediately as 'the Longbones'. Mercifully, there is no known record of how they thought of me, but I suspect that porky body and stubby little legs would come horribly close!

*Quite different from your average cat,*
*The Longbones have slim sculptured lines*
*With legs that make a stick look fat*
*And chiselled faces clean and fine.*
*Their ears are on the generous side,*
*And coats are close and trouble-free;*
*On long, slim paws they bounce and glide,*
*Occasionally running up a tree.*
*The Longbones love to play and leap*
*And roll around with catnip mice;*
*Exhausted, they will fall asleep*
*To dream of life in paradise.*
*But paradise looks just the same*
*As where they live, behind this door,*
*Because these cats, Longbones by name,*
*Have really landed on their paws.*

# CAT HOWARD

The little tortoiseshell cat seemed quite normal when I took her into the cat pens – well, as normal as any lively young tortie, which probably isn't all that normal actually. Some very dear friends had recently lost a much-loved Havana and had decided that a nice cuddly ginger boy would help to fill that dreadful gap left by Willow's departure.

One thing I soon learned about homing cats was that it didn't pay to be a slave to detail. An early triumph was to secure a home for an elderly black boy, who ended up happily ensconced with a couple who had thought they would like a tabby kitten. This confirmed my suspicions that people don't really know what they want and – rather like the mysterious chemistry that can suddenly happen between two humans – a certain look on a cat's face can turn the most emotionally stable person into a blubbering wreck. In that particular case, the couple ended up pleading with me to let them have 'Bluto' – and have remained entranced with him ever since.

When Carol and John asked if I had any ginger cats it seemed foolish not to promote the interests of the tortoiseshell girl, who was so close to being a ginger boy that the differences were hardly worth mentioning. The rest, as they say, is history. And indeed, history has taken over because in no time at all our little tortie traced her ancestry back to the time of the Tudors and instead of being called 'Molly' or 'Toffee', or even 'Mottle-Chops', she is now HRH Cat Howard – and jolly well makes the most of it.

*She is a naughty tortoiseshell*
*With royal lineage claimed;*
*Her family dates from Tudor times,*
*Hence the unusual name.*
*Her owners she regards as staff*
*To work and not complain*
*About the way she treats them,*
*With haughty, cold disdain.*
*Within the servant quarters*
*There's often muted moaning,*
*But Howard flicks her tail at them*
*And leaves them to their groaning.*
*So what if she is fussy –*
*They really should try harder:*
*Use more imagination*
*When stocking up the larder.*
*They seem think a royal cat*
*Should eat the same old stuff*
*As any lowlife moggy –*
*Common, loud and rough!*
*Don't they know how fortunate*
*They are to cook and clean*
*For HRH Cat Howard,*
*Who might one day be Queen?*

# CATS FROM THE WRONG SIDE OF THE TRACKS

We know only too well that caring for people and animals always makes you vulnerable, but it also brings huge rewards. It may be a suspect emotion, indicating all sorts of dangerous tendencies, but to take in a shivering, starving stray cat and see it blossom with veterinary care and good food is a heady experience and one which always moved me deeply.

Some people would say it shows a worrying neediness – a desire to 'play God', but the cat with the shining fur won't be bothered why you saved her; she'll just be pleased that someone did because she feels safe instead of frightened, warm instead of freezing cold and comfortably full instead of living with the pain and torment of starvation. She won't realise the implications of being spayed, but she has also been spared the trauma of raising litter after litter of fragile, undernourished kittens. While we have so many people who insist on playing the devil, it perhaps isn't such a bad thing that the rest of us at least try to act like decent human beings some of the time.

*These are the cats from the wrong side of the tracks.*
*They shot to the top of the housing list*
*With their mewling brood of mouse-like brats;*
*These are the cats from the wrong side of the tracks.*

*These are the cats who wear disgrace lightly.*
*They have tears in their ears and scuffed, dirty claws*
*And scratches on noses and deep scars from biting;*
*These are the cats that wear disgrace lightly.*

*These are the cats who have seen almost everything.*
*They sleep with the sun warming their bodies*
*And they don't care too much about anything.*
*These are the cats who have seen almost everything.*

*These are the cats who at last can sit dreaming.*
*Let the old cat woman bring them the good times,*
*An end to the starving and fighting and breeding.*
*These are the cats who at last can sit dreaming.*